FLITWICK:

A DAILY TONIC

By Keith Virgin

This book is dedicated to **G, H and J**
the daily tonic and inspiration for its completion.

In memory of Emily
(1984-2001)
A life so fragile, cherished forever.

First published October 2002
by
The Book Castle
12 Church Street
Dunstable
Bedfordshire LU5 4RU

© Keith Virgin 2002

ISBN 1-903747-23-6

The right of Keith Virgin to be identified as Author of this work has been asserted by him in accordance with the Copyright, Designs and Patents Act, 1988.

Typeset by the author.

Printed by Pear Tree Press, Stevenage

With acknowledgements to:
The Bedfordshire Times, County Records Office and Ordnance Survey. Ampthill and District Archaeological and Local History Society for two photographs from "A Vanishing Village."

All pictures are from the author's own collection, with the exception of those reproduced by kind permission of: J. Feazey, J. Lowe, K. Phelan, A. Swain and D.Young.

Front cover: Advertisement for Flitwick Water adapted from a painting by Thomas Gainsborough

Introduction

The parish of Flitwick lies at the heart of Bedfordshire between the towns of Bedford and Luton. It is, on the surface, little different from many other commuter towns which have grown up around a railway station: large housing estates, busy roads and crowds of commuters – a far cry from the village life of 100 years ago. Closer investigation, however, reveals evidence of that quieter existence: clusters of cottages around farmland, now engulfed by buildings; the old mill by the stream and the parish church standing at the edge of the community of which it was once the focus.

The moor is one of Flitwick's greatest attractions, it is also the keeper of a less commonly known historic fact – Flitwick was once the toast of many as yielding 'the most invigorating tonic in the world'.

Derived from the Saxon 'a dwelling by the stream', Flitwick evolved along the River Flit, flowing through the southeastern boundary of the parish and into Flitwick Moor to the east. At the side of the moor stood a house known as 'The Folly', occupied by one Henry King Stevens – a 'bird stuffer' by trade. Stevens became intrigued by the qualities of the water which bubbled up through the springs on his land. In the 1880s he began bottling the water and sold it for twopence a bottle. He took the step of having the medicinal qualities of the water recognised and achieved his aim in 1891 when the medical journal 'The Lancet' announced that Flitwick Chalybeate water had excellent qualities and was of the highest therapeutic value. It was advertised widely as 'An English medicinal spring, which yields the most invigorating tonic in the world'. To further attract custom, this proud boast was accompanied by a suitably adapted painting of 'The Cottage Girl' by Thomas Gainsborough, with Flitwick now engraved on the girl's pitcher. Unfortunately Stevens did not live to see the full extent of his enterprise before he died in1898, but the Flitwick Chalybeate Company was continued until the 1930s by R.W. White and co., the well- known soft drinks firm.

Henry King Stevens was laid to rest, alongside many of his contemporaries, in the churchyard of the parish church of St Peter and St Paul where the Reverend Frederick Bell Lipscomb had taken up office in 1894. The new vicar served the community for just five years before he met an untimely death after being knocked from his bicycle by a runaway horse. He did however leave to Flitwick a legacy which remains to this day; in January 1895 the Reverend Lipscomb produced the first Flitwick Parish Magazine.

Initially the magazine was introduced as a record of Church work, but it also gave space to matters of general parish life at the time. The Reverend Lipscomb's successor, the Reverend James Ledger Ward Petley took on his pastoral work with great zeal as well as bringing his own inimitable style to the parish magazine. In his twenty-seven years as vicar, the Reverend Petley took an active interest in village life and in 1911 published a book entitled 'Flitwick: The Story of an Old Bedfordshire Village'.

Flitwick entered the twentieth century as a village of just over one thousand inhabitants. It was divided into three ends with a railway station, opened in 1870, standing in almost splendid isolation at the centre of the parish. To the south was Church End, encompassing the church, manor house and village school. The church had stood at the top of Church Hill since Norman times surrounded by the grounds of Flitwick Manor, its nearest neighbour. The Brooks family inherited the Manor Estate in 1783 and remained there for three generations until 1934. John Thomas Brooks was responsible for landscaping the extensive grounds that made up the manor park. His son, John Hatfield Brooks inherited the estate, whilst another son, Thomas William Dell Brooks became vicar in 1855. It was he who was the overseer of two great restorations to the church in 1858 and 1867. On the death of her father in 1907 Catherine Brooks succeeded to the estate where she remained until her death in 1934. At the bottom of Church Hill, by the side of the village green and the pond, were the village school and schoolhouse. In 1872 the school took on Board School status under the leadership of Mr John Abbott who was headmaster there for forty years.

To the north of the station, straddling the road to Ampthill, was the fast-growing community known as Denel End with its Wesleyan Chapel built in 1873 and, until 1903, a windmill. The High Street had a variety of shops, public houses and newly built 'villas'. The east of the parish was known as East End and in 1908 a Baptist Church was built on land owned by Mr Richard Goodman of the family of millers who had lived at Flitwick Mill for three hundred years. The area around the station remained undeveloped until the turn of the century when 'substantial villas' were built in The Avenue, Station Square, The High Street, Steppingley Road and Kings Road.

Many of Flitwick's inhabitants found employment on farms in and around the parish, but others, like Henry King Stevens, of a more inventive or artistic temperament gained inspiration and income from their surroundings in other ways. Mr Alfred Pearse, an inventor of modest renown, moved into one of the new 'substantial dwellings' and Henry John Sylvester Stannard, a significant artist of the period, came to live in the village in 1894. He soon became a pillar of the community, organising and singing in concerts to raise funds for various causes, as well as being a member of local sports clubs.

Other villagers set up home in the small houses built around farms of the area. Typical of these was the Virgin family. Thomas and Kate née Pedder were married at the parish church on February 22nd 1905 and lived at 2 Chapel Road in Denel End for the next 60 years. Known locally as 'Paraffin Tom', Thomas sold paraffin and other house wares to neighbours in Flitwick and surrounding villages from his horse and cart. Kate had lived in Church Road, before entering into service for George Rushbrooke at St George's in nearby Ampthill. From here she made great use of a recent innovation in the world of communication-the picture postcard. For the cost of a half penny stamp a simple message could be written and posted in the morning, knowing that in most cases it would reach home later that same day. Views of even the smallest villages were reproduced on the front of these cards that were kept in albums in almost every home.

Throughout these times a great sense of community spirit prevailed. The annual village feast and sports day and other patriotic occasions provided great merriment and celebration. Events were organised to raise funds for various good causes. When the bells of the parish church needed re-hanging, a bazaar in the Manor Grounds was a resounding success, as was the sale of Mrs Petley's 'Flitwick Collection of Recipes'. Trips to the seaside and other outings provided opportunities for discovery and relaxation, whilst children from elsewhere were brought to Flitwick as a special treat. Clubs and societies were formed to bring villagers together, as well as encouraging competition against other local teams.

Despite the appearance of a simple, idyllic life-style, this was in fact a time of uncertainty and unrest. The century opened against the backdrop of the Boer War in far away South Africa and before twenty years had passed, the horrors of a world war had impacted on the lives of everyone.

This book attempts to capture the flavour of life in Flitwick, the folklore, customs and sights, which were so familiar at the beginning of the last century. It is also designed to serve as a permanent record of your own special anniversaries and memories in years to come. The pictures, news-items, poems and sayings are chosen to interest, inspire and soothe throughout the year. Like the Flitwick water, it is intended as a daily tonic.

"As a daily pick-me-up, one wineglass twice a day, morning and evening."

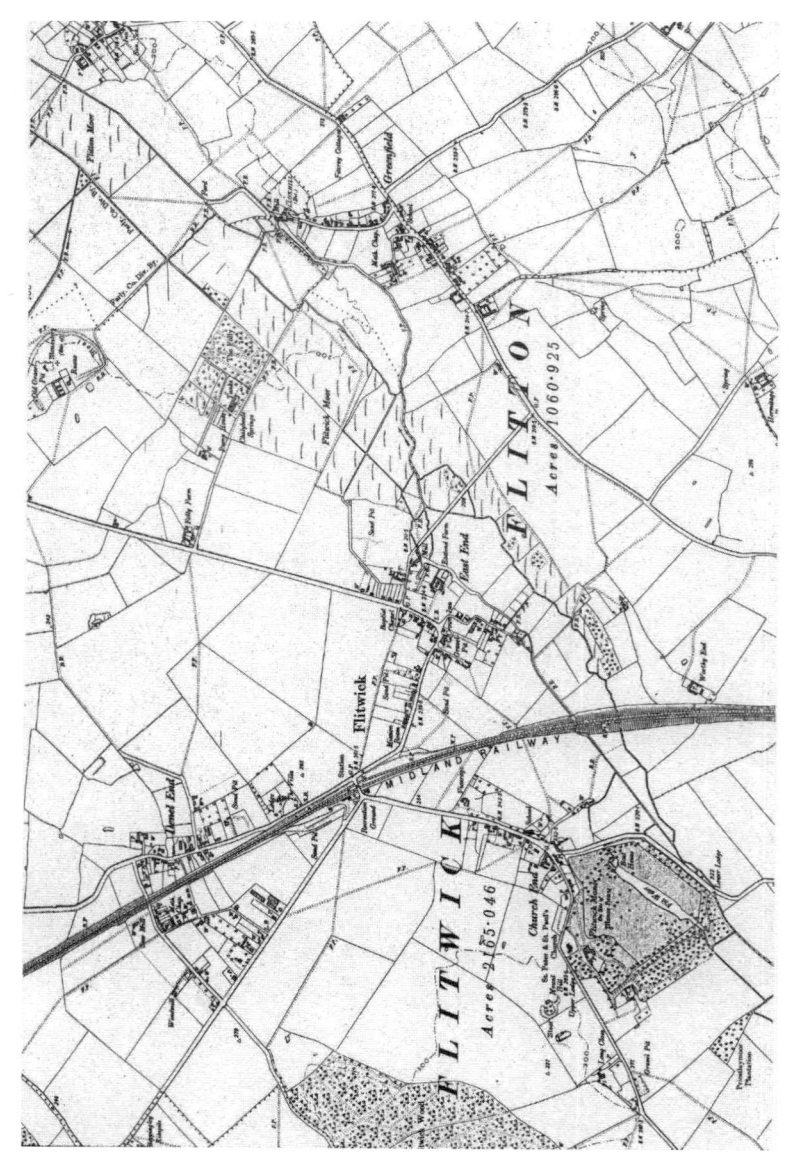

Flitwick 1901

January

"There was a time when meadow, grove, and stream,
The earth, and every common sight,
To me did seem
Apparelled in celestial light,
The glory and the freshness of a dream.
It is not now as it hath been of yore;
Turn wheresoe'er I may,
By night or day,
The things which I have seen I now can see no more."

William Wordsworth

January

1 New Year's Day

2

3

4

5 Twelfth Night

>   And I said to the man who stood at the gate of the year:
>   "Give me a light that I may tread safely into the unknown."
> And he replied: "Go out into the darkness and put your hand into the Hand
> of God. That shall be to you better than light and safer than a known way."
>
>   Minnie Louise Haskins

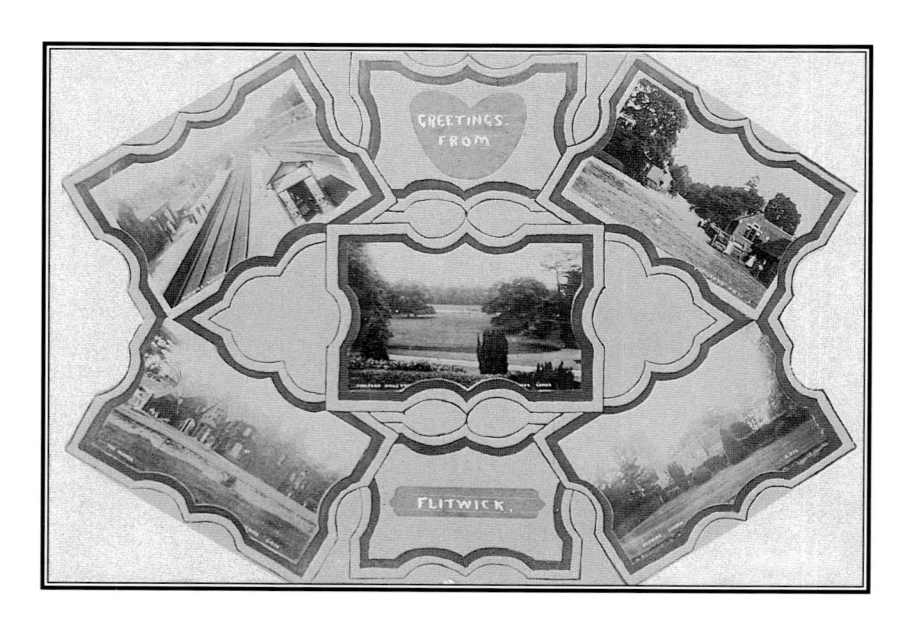

Dear Friends and Parishioners

Before this issue of the Parish Magazine is in your hands we shall have entered not only upon another year but another century. No longer shall we date our letters 18- as we have done all our lives but it will be 19-, and that for ever as far as we are concerned.

As a New Year comes in we are naturally led to consider the one that is past. When we come to a mile stone on Life's journey even the most thoughtless are wont to cast a backward glance along the path they have come and wonder what the unknown future has in store for them.

The New Year finds us as a Nation shrouded in gloom and sorrow owing to the terrible war now raging in South Africa. The past year has cast its own shadow over us as a Parish. Your beloved Vicar who has worked so hard on your behalf and for your good for the last five years has been taken away in the prime of his life, in the midst of his labours, without a moment's warning.

I come as a stranger in a strange land to fill his place and take up his work. I come to live in your midst to be your friend as well as your Minister and in health as well as in sickness I hope you will not find my friendship wanting.

J. L. WARD PETLEY.   *Parish Magazine 1900*

"And waiteth at the door.
There's a new foot on the floor, my friend
And a new face at the door, my friend
A new face at the door."

Epiphany 6

7

8

9

10

January

11 _____

12 _____

13 _____

14 _____

15 _____

Mr. Stannard's Concert

On the first evening of the New Year our School Room was more than packed with people eager to have some pleasant hours with Mr. Stannard and the accomplished performers, many being old favourites, that he always gathers round him on these annual occasions. But the room was not equal to the numbers that crowded for admission and after the porch had been pressed into service the rest had to go away. Of many of these, however, it would perhaps be more correct to say they stayed outside and if they could not hear much of music or song they would certainly gather from the loud and continual roars and shouts of merriment that reached them that those within were having a good time.

The proceeds were as usual on behalf of the poor and especially the widows of the parish.

Parish Magazine 1906

Choir Supper

On January 12th, the Choir-men were entertained to Supper at the Vicarage, and a pleasant evening was spent in games. A small electric battery was a special feature. Each one took his turn at the handles while the rest watched the very manifest results of the electric current and roared with laughter.

The Choir Boys were invited to tea at the Vicarage on January 18th, and a merry evening with games soon came to an end. The electric battery was again a great amusement.

Parish Magazine 1905

*"This is the way we go to school,
Go to school, go to school,
This is the way we go to school,
On a cold and frosty morning."*

_____ 16
_____ 17
_____ 18
_____ 19
_____ 20

January

21 _____

22 _____

23 _____

24 _____

25 *St Paul* _____

*"I call the living, mourn the dead,
I tell when days and years are fled;
For grief and joy, for prayer and praise,
To Heaven my tuneful voice I raise."*

The Church, Flitwick.

Our Church Bells

We have long known that they have been in a bad state, but only just recently an expert has said they are absolutely unsafe to ring.

We hereby give notice of a Public Meeting to be held in the Iron Room on January 8th, at 5 o'clock, to consider what can be done. We hope all who are interested in the Bells and like to hear their music ringing out on top of the hill, will come. We have sadly missed them this Christmas time, and the Old Year will die and the New Year be born without their heralding the event. We shall say no more now - for the present their ringing must cease; but if it is decided that a complete restoration shall take place, I fear there will have to be a good deal of noise made about the bells, before they can once more speak for themselves.

Parish Magazine 1909

"If St. Paul's Day be fair and clear
It doth betide a happy year
But if it change to snow or rain
Then will be dear all kinds of grain."

26

27

28

29

30

31

Kelly's Directory of Bedfordshire 1906

FLITWICK is a village and parish, bounded on the south by the Flitt, a tributary of the Ouse, with a station on the Midland railway, and is 3 miles south from Ampthill and 10 south from Bedford, in the Southern division of the county, hundred of Redbournestoke, petty sessional division, union and county court district of Ampthill, archdeaconry of Bedford and diocese of Ely. The church of SS. Peter and Paul is a small edifice of stone, in the Gothic style, restored and enlarged in 1858, and further improved in 1867, under the direction of Mr. W. Butterfield, architect: it consists of chancel, nave, aisles and an embattled tower containing 5 bells: on the north side is a Norman doorway: there are five memorial windows, one of which was erected in 1880 to the late Mrs Brooks, another was placed in 1885 by E. Jenkins esq. to his wife, a third in 1898 to the Rev. F. Ashpitel, vicar 1880-94, and a fourth in 1901 to the Rev. Frederick Bell Lipscomb M.A. vicar 1894-9: the oak reredos, erected in 1897, is a memorial to Mrs J.H. Brooks: the organ was presented by the late Mrs Brooks: the chancel was new-roofed in 1888 at the expense of Major Brooks J.P. The register dates from the year 1661. The living is a vicarage, net yearly value £170, including 45 acres of glebe, with residence, in the gift of Major Brooks, and held since 1899 by the Rev. James Ledger Ward Petley M.A. of St. John's College, Cambridge. At Denel End is an iron church, licensed by the Bishop, and seating 150, and at East End is an iron Mission room. There is also at Denel End a Wesleyan chapel, with 120 sittings, and at East End a small Baptist chapel, founded in 1660. A charity of £5 10s. yearly, arising from land known as "Poors Moor," is distributed in fuel: another charity, amounting to about £25 yearly and described as the "Town Lands Charity," is in part expended in fuel for the poor and the surplus is devoted to the outfitting of servant girls. Flitwick Manor House, the seat of Major John Hatfield Brooks D.L., J.P. is a mansion of brick, in a well-wooded and picturesque park containing a fine sheet of ornamental water. Major Brooks, who is lord of the manor, and the Duke of Bedford K.G. are the principal landowners. The soil is light gravel; subsoil, sand. The chief crops are wheat, oats, barley, beans and peas. The land is chiefly arable, comprising 2,159 acres of land and 6 of water; rateable value £9,071; the population in 1901 was 1,029.

Denel End and Flitwick East End are portions of this parish.
Sexton, George Scott.
Post, M. O. & T. O., S. B. & A. & I. Office. – Mrs. Rebecca Carr, sub-postmistress. Letters through Ampthill delivered at 7.5 & 12.30 a.m. ; dispatched at 10.15 a.m. & 5.55 p.m. No Sunday delivery of letters.
Wall Letter Box at East End, cleared at 10.25 a.m. & 6.5 p.m. ; at Denel End, cleared at 10.50 a.m. & 6.30 p.m. ; in Steppingley road, cleared at 10.35 a.m. & 6.15 p.m.
Council School (mixed & infants), enlarged in 1873 & again enlarged in 1893, & holding 200 children; average attendance, 207; John Abbott, master; Miss Katherine Gilson, infants' mistress.
County Police, Frederick Bushby, constable.
Railway Station, William George Hall, station master. *...continued at end of April*

February

How do I love thee? Let me count the ways.
I love thee to the depth and breadth and height
My soul can reach, when feeling out of sight
For the ends of Being and ideal Grace.
I love thee to the level of every day's
Most quiet need, by sun and candlelight.
I love thee freely, as men strive for Right;
I love thee purely, as they turn from Praise.
I love thee with the passion put to use
In my old griefs, and with my childhood's faith.
I love thee with a love I seemed to lose
With my lost saints, - I love thee with the breath,
Smiles, tears, of all my life! - and, if God choose,
I shall but love thee better after death.

Elizabeth Barrett Browning

February

1 _____

2 Candlemas _____

3 _____

4 _____

5 _____

"If Candlemas Day be fair and bright,
Winter will have another flight.
But if Candlemas Day be clouds and rain,
Winter is gone and will not come again"

Skating

Major Brooks has considerately placed his large fish pond at the disposal of the villagers for skating purposes, and this benefit has been made the most of during the last few days. A very nominal charge is made to indemnify the sweeper.

On Monday a little occurrence happened to mar the pleasure of the skaters. While one person was having skates put on, the man in attendance was driving the straps through with his knife when it suddenly clasped, taking off the top of his finger and the nail. He was given first aid on the spot, but the sight of blood, which flowed freely, upset the nerves of one young lady from Westoning, who promptly did a faint. Frozen snow was used as a restorative and her temples were freely rubbed with it, and at length, she gave signs of a recovery. The appearance of her features may be better imagined than described, as some of those who had assisted had not very clean hands.

So eager were some for the ice that they put in no less than eighteen hours on Monday, commencing at six in the morning.

Bedfordshire Times 1900

"Walk fast in snow,
In frost walk slow;
And still as you go,
Tread on your toe."

_____ 6

_____ 7

_____ 8

_____ 9

_____ 10

February

11

12

13

14 *St Valentine*

15

"Good morning, Valentine!
Curl your locks as I do mine,
Two before and three behind.
Good morning, Valentine."

The Jumble Sale

A Jumble Sale was held at the School on February 17th. The articles collected there were gathered from friends far and near by the energy of Miss Brooks and were of a truly miscellaneous character. It would be hard to mention many things that were not represented. Some few things were new but almost all were of the "have been" and "long ago" type. Like old soldiers some had seen plenty of active service yet were still ready and fit for a new campaign and very cheap at the price. As soon as the doors opened at 2.30 "everybody" came anxious to pick up a bargain and ready to find a use for the many "jumble" articles that were almost given away. The School-room was soon full and was kept up to crowding pitch till every stall was in the condition of Mother Hubbard's cupboard- bare.

Parish Magazine 1900

*"February fill dyke,
Be it black or be it white;
But if it be white,
It is better to like."*

_____ 16
_____ 17
_____ 18
_____ 19
_____ 20

February

21

22

23

24

25

*"If February brings no rain,
Tis neither good for grass nor grain."*

The Manor Grounds, Flitwick. 15276.

Death of Flitwick's Squire

Born May 20th 1824
Entered into Rest February 17th 1907
Interred February 21st 1907

It is with deep regret we have to chronicle the death of Flitwick's Squire, after many weeks of trying illness. We cannot but feel that a very part and parcel of Flitwick life has been taken from us, nor can we think of Flitwick Manor apart from him. It was here his earliest years were spent and here he has lived ever since his retirement from the Army now over 40 years ago, and here he passed away on the Sunday morning of February 17th. In 1843 he entered the Army, and his military career in India was a brilliant one, full of active service and dashing bravery in several of the well-known battles of that decade. He was also prominent in the Indian Mutiny and took part in various engagements for which he received numerous medals. On settling down at Flitwick he took a keen interest not only in all kinds of parochial matters but also in the wider interests of the County and the Diocese. In 1880 he was High Sheriff of the County, for many years the Chairman of the Ampthill Bench, a member of the Flitwick School Board during the whole of its existence, and chairman for the greater portion of the time. At Easter Vestry in 1866 he was appointed the Vicar's Churchwarden and has held that office ever since. His interest in Church matters was very great and he was ever ready to support any good work with his purse as well as his presence at Conferences, Meetings and on Committees.

Parish Magazine 1907

*Thirty days hath September, April, June and November,
All the rest have thirty-one, excepting February alone,
Which hath but twenty-eight days clear
And twenty-nine in each leap year.*

26

27

28

29

Bedfordshire Times & Independent 1901

Flitwick, which has an area of only a little over 2000 acres, is one of the few rural parishes in which the population shows a steady increase. This increase is due mainly to successful market-gardening and flower and fruit growing and to hat and bonnet sewing work from Luton. As a result of the market-gardening industry there is to be seen quite a new suburb of Flitwick on the north-west side of the railway, in the form of a multitude of decent small residences in the midst of large market-garden plots and extensive new orchards. Culture under glass too is conspicuous to the travellers by the Midland Railway. It will not be an altogether unexpected phenomenon if Flitwick should develop into a residential village. The air is salubrious, the soil gravelly and sandy and sites for "desirable mansions" are abundant. It is still remembered as part of the family traditions of old inhabitants that far back in the last century a medical man of wide repute resided at Flitwick and boarded rheumatic patients at his house from far and wide.

Every rural parish has a character of its own which can be recognised by the appreciative visitor, but cannot be given in words. One characteristic feature of Flitwick is the disjointedness of its groups of dwellings which makes the village extend over a great part of the parish. North of the railway station is Denel End, a rapidly growing district, in the olde portion of which are "The Blackbirds" and "The Wheatsheaf" licensed houses. The larger part of the population of Flitwick is, perhaps, to be found in the clusters of houses to the south-east of the railway station. Here most of the dwellings are of brick and slate, and look like the work of the nineteenth century. Here, too by the side of the little river Fleete or Flitt are the mill and residence of Mr. Richard Goodman. The mill is a "lineal descendant" of one that existed here before the Conquest and has been in possession of the family of the Goodmans for at least two centuries. Steam power has been added to that of water: but the place has happily not lost its old English picturesqueness. Half-a-mile beyond this is the tract of moor on which are the chalybeate springs. "The Crown" and "The White Horse" are in the East End of the parish. A third cluster of dwellings is to be found at some distance west of the railway station. Here are the vicarage, the board school —built in 1873 and since enlarged – "The Fir Tree" inn and higher up near the top of the hill, the church. On the south side of the church, divided from the churchyard only by the wall are the Manor House and park, the latter well timbered and dropping by gradual descent to the level of a fine piece of water. The house has an eighteenth century look about it, and is believed to occupy the site of a still older manor house. The Church End of the village is the most picturesque, and it is here that one comes upon more thatched and tiled and timber framed dwellings than in the other Ends. Artists are not unknown here; and I discovered that it was an artist that put up the German words, "Die Hutte", on a cottage door here. This designation has a pleasant suggestiveness of rustic Bohemianism – of a studio in a cottage.

March

I wandered lonely as a cloud
That floats on high o'er vales and hills,
When all at once I saw a crowd,
A host of golden daffodils;
Beside the lake, beneath the trees,
Fluttering and dancing in the breeze.

Continuous as the stars that shine
And twinkle on the milky way,
They stretched in never-ending line
Along the margin of a bay:
Ten thousand saw I at a glance,
Tossing their heads in sprightly dance.

William Wordsworth

March

1 *St David*

2

3

4

5

*"If March comes in like a lion,
It goes out like a lamb.
If it comes in like a lamb,
It goes out like a lion."*

The Flitwick Cookery Book

Having heard of several parishes where the following scheme has proved a great success, Mrs. Petley is anxious to start it here on behalf of the rehanging of the Flitwick Church Bells.
Subscribers are asked for on these terms.-
   I. Each to give 1/-.
   II. Each to contribute, if possible, one recipe.
   III. Each will receive a free copy of the book, containing all these recipes and others when printed.

If well taken up, as we have no doubt it will be, the Flitwick Cookery Book will not only yield a good profit to the Bell Fund but form a real help in many households. It will be, we venture to think, of more use than the average cheap books on the subject, containing as it will in its recipes what has been found by the experience of many to be the most practical and giving the best results.

Will all those interested in the matter and anxious to make this scheme the success we hope for, kindly bring it to the attention of some of their friends at a distance by sending to them one of these circulars, which can be obtained at the vicarage. Recipes and subscriptions (1/-) to be sent to Mrs. Petley, Flitwick Vicarage, Ampthill, not later than March 31st.

Parish Magazine 1909

*"Upon St David's day,
Put oats and barley in the clay."*

_____ 6

_____ 7

_____ 8

_____ 9

_____ 10

March

11 _____

12 _____

13 _____

14 _____

15 _____

"A windy March foretells a fine May."

Pancakes

Half lb. flour, a pinch salt, 1pint milk, 2 eggs (more if required). Put ½ lb. flour into basin, make hollow in centre and drop in the yolks of 2 unbeaten eggs, and a tablespoonful or so of milk. Stir flour gradually down from the sides and adding from time to time more milk. When about ½ pint milk has been used altogether, having worked gradually all the time, beat the mixture well with a wooden spoon till it is a mass of air bubbles. Then work in about half a pint more milk in the same way, let batter stand for 1 or 2 hours before using. The whites of eggs whisked to a stiff froth should be stirred in lightly and quickly at the very last before using the batter. If richer mixture is required use double number of eggs and leave out a gill of milk. A pinch of salt should always be added to flour.

Cowslip Wine

To each gallon of water allow 3½ lb. loaf sugar. Boil for 20 minutes taking off the scum. When lukewarm add the juice of 1 lemon and 2 oranges, together with the rind, peeled very thin. To each gallon of water add 1 gallon of cowslips. Put in the cask 1 tablespoonful yeast and a small quantity of isinglass, stirring it every morning for a week.

The Flitwick Collection of Recipes

Mix a pancake,
Stir a pancake,
Pop it in the pan.

Fry the pancake,
Toss the pancake,
Catch it if you can.

Christina Rossetti

16

St Patrick 17

18

19

20

March

21

22

23

24

25 *Lady Day*

"*On Mothering Sunday, above all other,
Every child should dine with its mother.*"

Rents

The Trustees of the Town, Moorlands and Parish Charities will receive the yearly rents due at Lady Day at the Parish Room between the hours of 7 and 8 on March 26th. The Poor's Moor of about 10 acres rented by Mr. Thomas Ellis will be re-let at the parish meeting to be held on March 28th at 7.30. The Vicar will sit to receive the half-yearly Allotment Rents at the Parish room on Monday, March 26th, between 7 and 8 o'clock.

A Ladies' Work Party

Probably many ladies in the parish would welcome the opportunity of meeting together once a week, especially during Lent, to work for our brave Soldiers and Sailors and even more for the sorrowing wives and mothers and little ones they leave behind them, alas! in so many cases never to meet again this side of the grave. Mrs. Petley will be pleased with such a purpose in view, to hold a working party at the Vicarage on Wednesdays, beginning on March 7th, at 2.30. Ladies are asked to bring their own material and work of any kind each likes, as for the above named purpose a use will be found for anything. All are heartily invited.

Parish Magazine 1900

"*March winds and April showers,
Bring forth May flowers.*"

26

27

28

29

30

31

Mr. H. Sylvester Stannard, R.B.A.

An ideal Bohemian existence for an artist is life in a bungalow, especially when the existence is attended by subsistence or power to earn it, pleasantly and by paying court to that coy mistress - Art. Many who have passed along the footpath which forms a short cut from Flitwick Station into East End will have gazed with interest on a dwelling of uncommon style and colour, standing in its own little wilderness on the right side of the footway. This is where Mr. and Mrs. H. Sylvester Stannard have pitched their tabernacle, or rather, to give it its proper name, The Bungalow.

Artists look at the world with eyes that are not given to ordinary folk, and curiosity has prompted us to try to put on Mr. Stannard's spectacles in the hope of being able to survey the prospect as he sees it from the windows of his cosy apartments. Prim lawns, straight weedless paths, and the meretricious blaze of flower beds, are foreign to the artistic instinct. We have here just a carpet of lush turf, flanked by groups of nodding sunflowers and spires of hollyhock, bordered by a diamond lattice fence and a hawthorn bush here and there. Beyond is a wide expanse of cabbage land - and even cabbages give pleasing waves of colour - and of long fields of barley and rye, bounded by the distant trees of Ampthill, Maulden, Clophill and Flitton, with the wide open sky over all, against which are silhouetted the rustic figures that pass to and fro or toil in the fields. Mr. and Mrs. Stannard have had their habitation and studio built to their own fancy, and it is needless to comment on the skilful treatment of the interior arrangements - the simple and effective panelling of the walls, or the womanly deftness of the drapings in neutral-tinted fabrics. Everything falls naturally into its place, and there is nothing overdone. Many charming little landscapes, the work of Mr. Stannard's artist friends, adorn the walls of the rooms. Among the painters thus represented are Edward Brown, Tatton Winter, RBA, and Col.Baylay: there are also fine examples of Mr. Alfred Pearse's imaginative work in black and white.

Mr. Pearse had been living at Flitwick some years when he suggested to his friend, Mr. Stannard, that he might find life in a country village favourable to the pursuit of art. The neighbourhood abounds with pleasant lanes, old cottages, and wide moorlands, upon which the lights and shadows play, while varius atmospheric phenomona in the changing seasons may be studied from the spacious windows of Mr. Stannard's *atelier*. Flitwick moor and the lane down by the mill and on toward Greenfield have long been the happy hunting-grounds of those who would capture bits of nature in her varying moods. Our artist soon perceived his opportunities, since Mr. Stannard is essentially a student of Nature, with a rare discriminating faculty. His realistic productions may be seen on the walls of most first class exhibitions. They are not all sunlit landscapes, though he delights in the smiling aspects of Nature: but his pictures are often truthful studies in difficult lights, with softened effects characterised by delicacy of treatment.

Bedfordshire Times 1898

April

*"Oh, to be in England
Now that April's there,
And whoever wakes in England
Sees, some morning, unaware,
That the lowest boughs and the brushwood sheaf
Round the elm-tree bole are in tiny leaf,
While the chaffinch sings on the orchard bough
In England - now!"*

Robert Browning

April

1 *All Fools' Day*

2

3

4

5

The first of April, some do say,
Is set apart for All Fools' Day,
But why the people call it so,
Not I nor they themselves do know.

The Story of St. Andrew's Church

It is with feelings of deep thankfulness and satisfaction that we gaze upon our new Church now completed, and what is still more, paid for. Only seven months ago when our Mission House had to be given up, we were in doubt and anxiety as to what we ought to do. Then an Iron Church being decided upon in a public Vestry, we were busy discussing sites and plans, and wondering how even the lowest estimates could possibly be met.

A site 130ft. by 40ft. with frontage on the Windmill Road and just 150ft. off the main Ampthill road, was secured for the reasonable sum of £28 from Messrs. Thorne and Nash. Of all the sites available this seemed the most suitable, as being on the side of Denel End farthest from the Parish Church and where growth of the parish seemed likely to be. Subsequent events have perfectly justified our choice and point to the likelihood of St. Andrew's being at no distant time the very centre of a considerable colony.

April 8th was the day fixed for the Opening and Dedication, which was performed by the Ven. Archdeacon Bathurst, acting as the Bishop's Commissary. The Church was crowded, numbers being unable even to find standing room, and all seemed to follow the Service with earnestness and thankfulness.

Parish Magazine 1903

"If the first three days of April are foggy
Rain in June will make lanes boggy."

_____ 6

_____ 7

_____ 8

_____ 9

_____ 10

April

11
12
13
14
15

"The year's at the spring;
The day's at the morn;
Morning's at seven;
The hill-side's dew-pearled;
The lark's on the wing;
The snail's on the thorn;
God's in His heaven-
All's right with the world! "

Robert Browning

Boy Scouts

The Boy Scouts movement has been taken up for this district by Captain Hope and the following boys from Flitwick have been enrolled as members and their uniform supplied by public subscriptions - W. Harris, G. Peddar, W. Parker, H. Atkins, J. Wood, W. Jellis, J. Goddard, B. Smith, Reggie and Roland Carr Horace, Joseph and Nathaniel Martin, P. Lamb.

On Sunday, April 17th, nearly two thousand Boy Scouts attended a special service at St Paul's Cathedral. The Bishop of Kensington gave them a stirring address and said he trusted this movement would promote among them manliness, obedience, self-control and brotherly service. We trust it may be so with our Scouts. Here is a standard for them to aim at and needed lesson for all to learn.

Parish Magazine 1910

FLITWICK. — WESLEYAN CHAPEL.

"*April with both sunshine and showers,
Bring out all the wild flowers.*"

.... 16

.... 17

.... 18

.... 19

.... 20

April

21

22

23 *St George*

24 *St Mark*

25

*"April weather,
Rain and sunshine together."*

Happy Inspirations

In the *Golden Penny* for this week Mr. Alfred Pearse, the artist of Flitwick, has been interviewed by a *Golden Penny* man respecting his numerous inventions. Mr. Pearse has patented between 20 and 30 inventions. The ideas have come to him whilst asleep and directly he wakes up he draws the idea. A model yacht is one of his inventions, the hull is 3ft, 6in. long and 8 in. wide, the sails are larger than most boats and are made of very thin material so that the air passes through them. Mr. Pearse hopes to see it win the American Cup. The most important of his inventions is the "Cyclone Wheel" for bicycles, bath chairs, hansoms, &c. In the wheel the pneumatic part is in the centre and solid or cushion tyres are used. The object is to minimise the vibration in a cheaper way than pneumatic tyres; there will be no bursting or puncturing and the wheels can be fitted to any existing cycle or vehicle. The whole cycle weighs 22lbs. Mr. Pearse has also invented a new kind of boot, a new game called "Bagball," a new kind of drawing pin which grips the paper firmly but does not pierce it and is much cheaper than the ordinary one. A new rivet for cycle chains is to be made in connexion with a pivot chain, which will be as strong, but lighter than ordinary chains, and any link can be repaired or added. Mr. Pearse also proposes constructing a flying machine, with cycling power for aerial navigation; there are two wings and a specially shaped aluminium balloon or air chamber, the steering to be done by the wings. The balloon is attached to the lower framework by ropes.

Bedfordshire Times 1898

*"When April blows her horn,
It is good for hay and corn."*

26

27

28

29

30

Kelly's Directory of Bedfordshire 1906

Continued from January

Brooks Major John Hatfield D.L., J.P. — Flitwick Manor House
Hope Capt. James, — Hampden Lodge
Hubbard Stewart, — Long Close
Hunter Capt. J. Edward R.N. — The Hollies
Knuttel Frederick, — The Villa
Peak Mrs — The Avenue
Petley Rev. James Ledger Ward M.A. (vicar), — Vicarage
Seabrook Samuel, — Dengarth
Searle Mrs. — Canterbury Villa
Stannard Harry Sylvester

COMMERCIAL.

Abbiss, Edwin, farmer, Home farm
Abbott John, baker, Denel End
Barker & Feazey, butchers
Billington Bros., market gardeners
Billington Robert, market gardener
Brittian William, farmer, Wood farm
Carr George, butcher
Carr Wm., blacksmith, Church End
Cousins Charles, baker
Dawson Lincoln & Fred, drapers
Deacon Robert, horse dealer
Dickinson Geo., farmer, Ruxox farm
Dillingham Cecil, plumber & decortr
Dix Ebenezer, insurance agent & assistant overseer
Dix Emma (Mrs.), shopkeeper
Dix Peter, farmer, Little Farm
Dix William, sand merchant
Dudley Arthur, shopkeeper
Ellis Rebecca (Mrs.), beer retailer, East End
Feazey Walter, butcher, see Barker & Feazey
Flitwick Chalybeate Co (R. White & Co. proprietors), natural mineral springs, East End
Flitwick Coal Co. Limited
Franklin Charles, coal mer., Station
Frost William, builder
Fuller William G., grocer
Goodman Rd., miller (water & steam)
Hatcher George, Crown inn
Hawtin Arthur W., newsagent
Hill Thomas, carpenter, Windmill rd
Howard Susan (Mrs.), shopkeeper
Kingham Joseph, baker
Line Leonard & Son, chimney swprs
Line Daniel, chimney sweeper
Martin Eli, carpenter, builder & undertaker, East End
Martin Fred, brewers' agent
Martin Mary Ann (Mrs.), Blackbirds P.H.
National Deposit Friendly Society (Arthur W. Hawtin, sec)
Nutt Henry Wm., farmer, East End
Odell Wm. Geo., beer ret. Church End
Page Sophia (Mrs.), beer ret. Denel End
Pepper Edwin J., saw mills, Denel End
Phillips Edward, farmer, see Street & Phillips
Saunders Samuel, boot maker
Seabrook Samuel, farmer & landowner, Dengarth
Sharp Chas., mkt gdnr., Church End
Sharp George, poultry dealer
Sharpe Charles, builder & grocer
Short William, Swan inn, Station
Simms Joseph, shopkeeper
Stannard Harry Sylvester R.B.A., artist
Street & Phillips, farmers, Priestley farm
Tookey William, farmer, Denel End
Vincent Mary (Miss), dress maker, Windmill Road
Walters Richard, farmer, Folly farm
Washington Chas., frmr., Valley farm
Wilcocks Herbert F. A., cycle repairer
Wilson Albert, farmer, East End

May

Shall I compare thee to a summer's day?
Thou art more lovely and more temperate;
Rough winds do shake the darling buds of May,
And summer's lease hath all too short a date;
Sometime too hot the eye of heaven shines,
And often is his gold complexion dimmed,
And every fair from fair sometime declines,
By chance, or nature's changing course, untrimmed;
But thy eternal summer shall not fade,
Nor lose possession of that fair thou ow'st,
Nor shall Death brag thou wand'rest in his shade,
When in eternal lines to time thou grow'st:
So long as men can breathe, or eyes can see,
So long lives this, and this gives life to thee.

William Shakespeare

May

1 *May Day*

2

3

4

5

The fair maid who, the first of May
Goes to the fields at break of day
And washes in dew from the hawthorn tree,
Will ever after handsome be.

Local Success

We are pleased to hear that the promising young artist, Mr H. Sylvester Stannard, R.B.A., has been successful in this year's Royal Academy, which opens on May 1, with his water colours. He sent up four landscapes of Flitwick and the immediate vicinity, all of which were accepted and hung. One of them, the largest, was a very natural effect of stormy weather on an open country, in which a man was carting mangold wurtzels, his title for the picture being "Wurzel time in Bedfordshire." Another of the selections we might mention was a very tranquil evening scene of the moors, in which his sunsets always find prominence. Flitwick has never before been shown in the Royal Academy to the extent it has during the few years Mr. Stannard has resided in its midst.

Bedfordshire Times 1899

Now the bright Morning star, day's harbinger,
Comes dancing from the East, and brings with her
The flowery May; who from her green lap throws
The yellow Cowslip and the pale prim-rose
Hail! bounteous May that dost inspire
Mirth and youth and warm desire.
Woods and groves are of thy dressing
Hill and dale doth boast thy blessing
Thus we salute thee with our early song
And welcome thee and wish thee long.

John Milton

_____ 6

_____ 7

_____ 8

_____ 9

_____ 10

May

11 _____

12 _____

13 _____

14 _____

15 _____

Mist in May, heat in June,
Makes the harvest come right soon.

Houses For Sale

The sale by auction by Messrs. G. A. Wilkinson and Son in conjunction with Messrs. Swaffield and Son, at the White Hart Hotel, Ampthill, of the freehold building plots opposite the Midland Station, and fronting the main road, took place on the 5th, but did not elicit a purchaser, though we understand that negotiations are going on privately. In making it conditional that dwelling-houses of a certain value should be erected, the owner no doubt acted very wisely, and in the best interest of the town, especially as we understand other land can be added (very reasonably) to each lot if desired. No doubt there are disadvantages in trying to get single individuals to build larger houses than have been put up recently, but it is generally thought that such are needed, and there appears to be a feeling that if a small local company could be formed to select a suitable piece of land and to build say half a dozen houses, standing on about 1 or 1? acres of ground, to let at £60 to £70 a year, the place might reasonably be expected to advance, and a good return on the outlay would be received. Several enquiries have been made for such a class of house during the past few months.

Bedfordshire Times 1902

Spud a thistle in May, it will come another day
Spud a thistle in June, it will come again soon
Spud a thistle in July, it will surely die.

16

17

18

19

20

May

21
___

22
___

23
___

24
___

25
___

The Sun doth arise, *The birds of the bush*
And make happy the skies; *Sing louder around*
The merry bells ring *To the bells' cheerful sound,*
To welcome the Spring; *While our sports shall be seen*
The skylark and thrush, *On the Echoing Green.*

William Blake

The Cricket Club

On June 3rd, a meeting was held to consider the possibility of starting a Cricket Club. The number of those present was not large, but all were enthusiastic. It was finally arranged that a Club should be immediately started, and a number of names were suggested as officers. Mr. Knibbs was appointed Hon. Secretary and Treasurer, and will be glad to receive any subscriptions or donations. Mr C. Sharpe very kindly offered to lend some tools to commence with till funds admitted of the Club buying their own. Matches are already being arranged and we wish them all success.

The new Club has already got to work and its numbers are growing. A single innings match was played between Married and Single on July 5th which resulted in a win for the married. The score being Married 45, Single 28. For the former, F. Briden, F. Dawson, W Carr, W. Baker were the chief run getters. For the latter, M. Crawley, S. Short, A. Webb. Short and Stacey for the Single, and Briden for the Married, did most with the ball.

On Feast Monday, July 18th, a match was played on our ground with Pulloxhill and resulted in a win for us by a wicket and one run. F. Briden was captain and Sergeant Kitchener Umpire.

Parish Magazine 1904

"Button to chin, till May be in
Ne'er cast a clout, till May be out."

_____ **26**

_____ **27**

_____ **28**

_____ **29**

_____ **30**

_____ **31**

In Memoriam

THOMAS WILLIAM DELL BROOKS.

Born April 13th, 1828. Entered into Rest May 4th, 1908.

Interred at Bedford Cemetery, May 8th.

It is with deep regret we take our last farewell of one who has for so long and so intimately been connected with our Parish. The third son of John Thomas Brooks, Esq., of Flitwick Manor, he belonged to us by birth. Our Baptismal Registers contain this entry:-

Sept. 8th 1828. Thomas William Dell, son of John Thomas and Mary Brooks, Esq., Flitwick Gentleman. George Cardale, Vicar.

In the Font we use was he baptised. In the Church for which he was destined, when grown a man, to do so much, he worshipped as a boy. In the parish to which he gave the best years of his life, was his home. In 1855 he was presented by his Father to the Living of Flitwick, which he held until 1880. During his 25 years Incumbency he did more for the Church and Parish than probably any other Vicar ever did. As to the Church, the great Restoration of 1858 was due to his zeal and energy, as also the completion of that Restoration in 1867. The Church having been put into proper repair, with necessary improvements and additions, such as the North Aisle and Vestry, he turned his attention to the improvement of the Services. Then in 1864 the Churchyard was enlarged. The value of the Living was considerably increased by his draining the Moors and making what was swamp possible for allotments. Improvements to the School and the building of the School House were due to him. The Parish at large and in fact all the surrounding Parishes owe him no small debt of gratitude for the part he took in the making of the "New Road" connecting up two main roads by a cross cut and thus saving miles of "going round." We scarcely realize that less than 50 years ago there was no road there. Having done so much for the good of the church and the Parish, he turns his attention to the Vicarage, all too small, for any average family, and enlarges and improves it. Many of the beautiful trees which form such a pleasant setting to it were planted by him. In quiet simple life and earnest sympathy with those around him, the 25 years sped by. The old folk who can remember so far back still speak fondly of "Parson Brooks" and his work.

Parish Magazine 1908

June

Yes. I remember Adlestrop –
The name, because one afternoon
Of heat the express-train drew up there
Unwontedly. It was late June.

The steam hissed. Someone cleared his throat.
No one left and no one came
On the bare platform. What I saw
Was Adlestrop – only the name

And willows, willow-herb, and grass,
and meadowsweet, and haycocks dry,
No whit less still and lonely fair
And the high cloudlets in the sky.

And for that minute a blackbird sang
Close by, and round him, mistier,
Farther and farther, all the birds
Of Oxfordshire and Gloucestershire.

Edward Thomas

June

1 ⎯⎯⎯⎯⎯⎯⎯⎯⎯⎯⎯⎯⎯⎯⎯⎯⎯⎯⎯⎯⎯⎯⎯⎯⎯⎯⎯⎯⎯⎯⎯⎯⎯⎯

2 ⎯⎯⎯⎯⎯⎯⎯⎯⎯⎯⎯⎯⎯⎯⎯⎯⎯⎯⎯⎯⎯⎯⎯⎯⎯⎯⎯⎯⎯⎯⎯⎯⎯⎯

3 ⎯⎯⎯⎯⎯⎯⎯⎯⎯⎯⎯⎯⎯⎯⎯⎯⎯⎯⎯⎯⎯⎯⎯⎯⎯⎯⎯⎯⎯⎯⎯⎯⎯⎯

4 ⎯⎯⎯⎯⎯⎯⎯⎯⎯⎯⎯⎯⎯⎯⎯⎯⎯⎯⎯⎯⎯⎯⎯⎯⎯⎯⎯⎯⎯⎯⎯⎯⎯⎯

5 ⎯⎯⎯⎯⎯⎯⎯⎯⎯⎯⎯⎯⎯⎯⎯⎯⎯⎯⎯⎯⎯⎯⎯⎯⎯⎯⎯⎯⎯⎯⎯⎯⎯⎯

When June is come, then all the day
I'll sit with my love in the scented hay:
And watch the sunshot palaces high,
That the white clouds build in the breezy sky.

Robert Bridges

Flitwick Station

The Choir Outing

Soon after five o'clock we were all on the platform, and when the special train drew up we quickly scrambled into our reserved compartments and were on our way to Hastings. It was a lovely, if a somewhat long run through beautiful country in the cool of the morning. The hop-fields of Kent, "The Garden of England" were new to many and were eagerly scanned. An excellent dinner and tea were landmarks in a long day. In the full blast of a heat wave and at a spot which holds the record for sunshine, we had no difficulty in keeping warm, and breaking up into small parties we spread abroad in various directions and with a variety of aims. There was something to satisfy every taste, except cooling shade of which there did not seem enough to go round. The "Joy Wheel" was certainly deserving of its reputation as causing unlimited merriment and laughter, and most of our party found their way there sooner or later. At 7.30 we began the homeward journey. To the loud accompaniment of music, both vocal and instrumental, as the concert bills say, which rolled up and down the long train and poured forth from every open window, the engine puffed on. The minimum of clothing was the order of the day. To say everyone was hot, including the train itself, was to put it mildly. As the hours passed by enthusiasm slackened somewhat. There appeared to be a greater tendency to meditate than to sing. After creeping through the under-ground London, even meditation seemed too much, and a great silence prevailed. It is the last and general stage of a long trip, especially when a "Heat-wave" is on. A happy yet tired party stood once more on Flitwick platform and one and all wish to thank all those who helped give them their day's outing.

Parish Magazine 1912

June

11
12
13
14
15

Winter is cold-hearted,
Spring is yea and nay,
Autumn is a weathercock
Blown in every way.
Summer days for me
When every leaf is on its tree.

Christina Rossetti

A Balloon

Just about tea time on Sunday, June 15th, the appearance of a large balloon with a car containing two men filled us with a mild excitement. Even had it been its intention of giving us a good exhibition it could not have done better, for as it neared Flitwick it dropped lower and lower, and apparently caught by different currents of air, it sailed round and round so close to the ground that the trailing rope could be easily reached. But when some attempted to take hold of it the gentlemen in the car of the balloon made it very clear by their forcible and emphatic remarks that they did not wish to be hauled down! It then sailed gracefully and slowly by the Vicarage and so low down that it had some difficulty in getting away because of the height of the trees, and then, gradually rising to a great height, disappeared in an easterly direction.

Parish Magazine 1913

CHURCH END, FLITWICK.

*"June damp and warm
Does the farmer no harm."*

.... 16
.... 17
.... 18
.... 19
.... 20

June

21

22

23

24 Midsummer Day, St John

25

*"Calm weather in June
Sets the corn in tune."*

Sunday School Excursion

Half-past four o'clock and a fine morning! So said many on June 30th. A little later they were all on the way to the station, and our special reserved carriages which we had booked from Harlington, were all that we could want, and there was no crushing nor confusion, either going or returning.

From us to Yarmouth is a long way, but with eating our breakfast, or rather consuming the provisions we had brought with us, and taking a keen interest in everything we saw, the hours passed quickly, and we duly arrived at the sea and "the sands." There was plenty to do, and a day, or rather a part of a day of cloudless sunshine to do it in. There was something to appeal to every taste, and all seemed happy. We gathered for tea at 5 o'clock and each teacher reported the little flock entrusted to his or her care was safe and sound. After thoroughly enjoying our shrimps we started for the station, and at 6.30 were on the homeward way, mostly very tired, but yet well content. The bonfires we looked out for and saw, or thought we saw, helped to amuse us, and kept some awake that might otherwise possibly have been asleep. We stepped out on a soaking platform and walked home at midnight on wet roads, and felt glad that the rain we needed had come while we were away.

Parish Magazine 1902

"A swarm of bees in May is worth a load of hay,
"A swarm of bees in June is worth a silver spoon,
A swarm of bees in July is not worth a fly."

26

27

28

St Peter 29

30

Our Summer Outing

June 22nd! Why it was actually a fine morning, and still more, with every promise of a fine day. It seemed almost too good to be true, and we all rejoiced accordingly.

By five o'clock a larger crowd had gathered at our station than had been seen there for many a year. Men and women, boys and girls, many with parcels, which truth to tell mostly contained breakfast, all with happy faces and eager enquiry. At quarter past, the long special train which the Vicar had arranged for steamed in, and in about ten minutes all the various parties were comfortably settled in their reserved carriages and bound for Lowestoft.

At Ampthill two more parties joined us and Rev. W.C. Browne drove in to Bedford all the way from Haynes with his choir to pick us up there. No more stops were now made except so far as signals compelled, and though it was a far cry from Bedford to Lowestoft, which we reached at about 11, yet the journey afforded a great deal of fun and was far from being regarded as lost time, especially by the younger members of the party.

Our own party which numbered over 100, was composed of the elder Sunday School children and Sunday School teachers, the Choir, Miss Brooks' classes and Mr. Abbott's Night School Boys. Then of course there were a number of others besides. Mr. Lowings alone had something like 20 of his own friends. Choirs and clergy, &c., from Westoning, Clophill, Greenfield, and Houghton Conquest also joined us, making up altogether a long and well-filled train.

Lowestoft was new ground to the majority, and it stood the test of the naturally severe criticism that was brought to bear upon it. All seemed delighted at the selection. The fishing fleet and the sale of their fish in the tremendous auction markets was a novel and pleasing sight. Of course there were the usual seaside delights, the beach with its fun, the paddling, the trip on the water, too often with its usual sad consequences as eloquently told by pale faces and mournful expressions on the return.

Nor was the dinner forgotten, nor the great trooping at 6 of weary feet for tea and the shrimps which must never be omitted. Then the station rush and the searching for the special carriages, the checking of lists to see all were there, the starting (7.15 p.m. o'clock) with many voices raised in song or cheer, and then a gradual settling down for the journey. In many a carriage all was quiet, for many slept. At 12.30 all were awake and making tracks for home. A successful day, and we are glad.

Parish Magazine 1903

July

"Faster than fairies, faster than witches,
Bridges and houses, hedges and ditches;
And charging along like troops in a battle,
All through meadows the horses and cattle;
All of the sights of the hill and the plain
Fly as thick as driving rain;
And ever again, in the wink of an eye,
Painted stations whistle by.

Here is a child who clambers and scrambles,
All by himself and gathering brambles;
Here is a tramp who stands and gazes;
And there is the green for stringing the daisies!
Here is a cart run away in the road
Lumping along with man and load;
And here is a mill, and there is a river:
Each a glimpse and gone forever!"

Robert Louis Stevenson

July

1 _____

2 _____

3 _____

4 _____

5 _____

*"When the dew is on the grass,
Rain will never come to pass"*

The Girls' Friendly Society

The members of the Flitwick and Ampthill Branch of the G.F.S. comprising 12 parishes, held their Annual Festival this year on July 20th, at Flitwick Manor, by the kind invitation of Major and Miss Brooks. It was a charming spot to wander about, and the justly famed trees of the Manor Grounds afforded welcome shade. A Ladies Band from Bedford played for some hours in the natural amphi theatre in front of the house, and many danced merrily away to its strains. The other lawns were taken up with various round games, especially dear to girls. Tea was served by Mr. Kingham of Flitwick, in the Lime Avenue, and no more charming spot could have better set off the well-laden tables and the bright dresses of the 170 "Friendly Girls" and Associates that sat down to them.

Parish Magazine 1904

"The summer sun is sinking low;
Only the tree-tops redden and glow;
Only the weather-cock on the spire
Of the village church is a flame of fire;
All is in shadow below."

H. W. Longfellow

July

11 _____

12 _____

13 _____

14 _____

15 *St Swithin* _____

"St Swithun's Day if thou dost rain,
For forty days it will remain;
St Swithun's Day if thou be fair,
For forty days 'twill rain no mair."

Thunderstorm

A terrific thunderstorm burst over us just about the time of the Evening Service on Sunday July 19th. We deeply regret that the old Vicarage was struck by lightning and a good part of the house wrecked. Worst of all, Mr. W. Carr was near that part of the house at the time, and was rescued in an unconscious condition. Grave fears were at first entertained for his complete recovery, but now we are thankful to say there is every hope that in a while he will be quite well again. The sincere sympathy of all goes out to Mr. and Mrs. Carr in this calamity, and in the terrible shock they have experienced. The thought of what might have been fills us with a great and heartfelt thankfulness to Almighty God for His merciful preservation.

Parish Magazine 1903

THE OLD LODGE. FLITWICK MANOR.

*"A shower in July,
When the corn begins to fill,
Is worth a plow of oxen,
And all belongs there till."*

16

17

18

19

20

July

21

22

23

24

25

*"In July, some reap rye,
In August, if one will not, the other must."*

The Holiday Home Children

As the three o,clock train from London steamed in on July 31st, twenty-four bright happy little faces tried to look out of the same carriage window all at once. Soon were they all on the platform with their belongings which were done up in every variety and every shape of box and bag and parcel. The Vicar, who is country correspondent for Flitwick, read the labels attached to each and having checked their names marched them off to the Recreation Ground where a selected number of Mothers were awaiting them. At the invitation of the Vicar and Mrs Petley, they spent a pleasant afternoon at the Vicarage on August 11th.

Their fortnight went all too quickly and on August 14th we again all met at the station, bag and baggage this time largely increased by country produce, flowers, &c., each receiving a bag of sweets as they said goodbye.

Parish Magazine 1900

"He who bathes in May,
Will soon be laid in clay.
He who bathes in June,
Will sing a merry tune.
He who bathes in July,
Must dance till he is dry."

_____ 26

_____ 27

_____ 28

_____ 29

_____ 30

_____ 31

The Village Feast

Flitwick was, on Monday, in gala garb. The village feast is a red-letter day in the life of the inhabitants. This time-honoured institution goes back to pre-Reformation, a circumstance which explains its occurrence within the octave of the festival of the patron saint of the Church. Hence we may observe *en passant* the common origin of the English rural "feast" and the continental *festa*. A better date for a *fete champetre* could not be selected. It is a season when the country is looking its loveliest. It is a time of abundant fruits, of ripening corn, of deep lush grass, and when a gipsy existence is possible with or without tents. Even a casual visitor notes that Flitwick is a parish of fat meads, pleasant pastures, and sylvan glades of charming picturesqueness, while away yonder bubbles the village stream, recalling Coleridge's verse:-

>A noise like a hidden brook
>In the leafy month of June,
>That to the sleeping woods all night
>Singeth a quiet tune.

Along the brook's banks are wild flowers and aquatic plants, while among its shallows dart the water wagtails, "sipping 'twixt their jerking dance." Amid scenes and sounds such as these Flitwick on Monday kept high festival. The poets tell us that the world as it grows old returns to its early loves. Hence it is not surprising to find that the rustic simplicity of Flitwick shows a marked preference for such primitive pastimes as merry-go-rounds, swing boats, shooting galleries and cocoa-nut shies.

These attractions were located in the Recreation Ground, and were very extensively patronised. Mr. Stannard gave a clever exhibition of marksmanship with a Winchester repeater, much to the admiration of the visitors. It was quite exhilarating to observe with what zest one and all the parishioners, irrespective of rank or class, entered into the fun of the feast.

Athletic sports were organised by a Committee, consisting of the Rev. F. Lipscombe, Capt. Stretton, and Messrs. W. Baker, Hobbs, Dawson, Feazey, Nutt, Sylvester Stannard, and R. Billington, most of whom gave prizes. One of the most interesting features of the day's proceedings was a cricket match, Flitwick v. Silsoe.

The various amusements were kept up until a late hour. The happy scene presented by the rustic festival was a picturesque portrayal in real life of Goldsmith's familiar lines-

>All the village train from labour free
>Led up their sports beneath the spreading tree,
>While many a pastime circled in the shade,
>The young contending as the old survey'd;
>And many a gambol frolick'd o'er the ground,
>And sleights of art and feats of strength went round;
>And still, as each repeated pleasure tired,
>Succeeding sports the mirthful band inspired!

Bedfordshire Times 1898

August

"What is this life if, full of care,
We have no time to stand and stare?

No time to stand beneath the boughs
And stare as long as sheep and cows.

No time to see, when woods we pass,
Where squirrels hide their nuts in grass.

No time to see, in broad daylight,
Streams full of stars, like skies at night.

No time to turn at Beauty's glance,
And watch her feet, how they can dance.

No time to wait till her mouth can
Enrich that smile her eyes began.

A poor life this if, full of care,
We have no time to stand and stare."

W. H. Davies

August

1 *Lammas*

2

3

4

5

*"If the first week in August is unusually warm,
the winter will be white and long."*

The Coronation Festivities August 9th

Flitwick was at its gayest on Saturday. As the morning opened with bright sunshine, Union Jacks, bunting and various other patriotic decorations were to be seen fluttering in the breeze throughout the town. Mr. E. Abbiss had very kindly lent his large field for the occasion. Outside the School-house were the letters "E" and "R" in large gilt, with a crown between, and these were tastefully set off with a long strip of bunting and Union Jacks. The entrance to the Schoolroom was gaily decorated.

Of the sports, which occupied the whole of the afternoon and most of the evening, the most exciting and amusing item was the donkey race. There were 7 entries, S.A. Stephen's "King Edward" (jockey, C. Nutt); Line's (jockey, J. Ellis); and W. Carr's (ridden by owner), coming home in the order named. As the start was given the donkeys got mixed up, and soon most of the riders were on the ground. Mr. Stringer's donkey threw Master Abbiss over its head, a distance of 5 yards, and made off, but was caught by its rider, who again mounted; both of the donkeys ridden by Messrs. Barnes and Beal laid down; W. Britton's donkey (Sceptre), ridden by himself, also laid down, W. Carr's following its example. The winner, "King Edward," seeing the course eventually clear, made off and was three times round the course before the others had traversed it once. By means of sundry efforts in pushing, coaxing etc., the other winners reached the end of the journey.

Parish Magazine 1902

"The English winter ends in July and starts again in August."

August

11
___

12
___

13
___

14
___

15
___

> *"Monday's child is fair of face,*
> *Tuesday's child is full of grace.*
> *Wednesday's child is full of woe,*
> *Thursday's child has far to go.*
> *Friday's child is loving and giving,*
> *Saturday's child works hard for his living.*
> *The child that is born on the Sabbath Day,*
> *Is fair and wise, good and gay."*

Harvest Holidays

Our Schools broke up for the Harvest Holidays on August 10th, and will open again on September 14th. In the meanwhile Brush and Broom will be the order of the day inside, while outside the Infants' playground will be levelled according to the suggestion of the Inspector, which will make play easier and happier on the little feet.

Mr. Abbott is passing his well deserved holiday in Northumberland where he will have abundant opportunities of revisiting old haunts that are dear to him and of enjoying his favourite recreation of fishing. We wish him a happy time and much luck in tempting the wily trout to exchange their native streams for a place in his creel.

Parish Magazine 1900

"The coach is at the door at last;
The eager children, mounting fast
And kissing hands, in chorus sing:
Good-bye, good-bye, to everything!"

Robert Louis Stevenson

_____ 16

_____ 17

_____ 18

_____ 19

_____ 20

August

21

22

23

24 *St Bartholomew*

25

*"If the twenty-fourth of August be fair and clear,
Then hope for a prosperous autumn that year."*

Mothers' Meeting Tea

On August 21st, Mrs Petley invited the members of her Mothers' Meeting to tea at the Vicarage. In spite of threatenings the rain kept off so that tea on the lawn was pleasant. This over, all were grouped together and a photograph was taken of them by Mrs Jago. As "Spot" (the Vicarage dog) was never absent from a single Meeting, it was only right she should take her place in the group, which she seemed pleased to do.

Swings and various games passed the time quickly away. Then the races, especially the needle and the egg and spoon race, caused much amusement.

The Tug of War proved the ladies' muscles to be in good order, certainly too good for the ropes which broke again and again under the strain placed upon them.

At 7.30 we realised that the days were drawing in so we sang "God Save the Queen" and said "Good Night."

Parish Magazine 1900

*"A rainy August
Makes a hard bread crust."*

_____ 26

_____ 27

_____ 28

_____ 29

_____ 30

_____ 31

The Bazaar for the Flitwick Church Bells

Our Bazaar is past and gone and we cannot but look back to it, for when we planned and worked so long and so diligently, but with feelings of deep gratitude and not a little satisfaction at its great success.

The idea originated with Miss Brooks. She very kindly offered the Manor grounds, so pretty and so suitable and with such a setting one feature of success was assured at the very beginning. The seed of a "Garden Fete" side by side with the Bazaar was sown in good soil and soon sprang up a lusty plant, for a "Garden Fete" and a "Bazaar" are quite regarded in this district as inseparable.

A Band from Bedford was engaged. Two concerts by some of the Strolling R.N.s were kindly offered by Mr. A.C. St V. Bannister, their leader and readily accepted and which were most excellent. A Bicycle Gymkhana was arranged for the afternoon and another one for the evening by Mr. Davis, both of which caused great amusement, prizes being offered by various ladies and gentlemen. A coconut shy was well placed in the hands of Mr. Gibbons and brought in a larger legitimate percentage of profit than many other things might have done. A Hat Trimming competition for men in the hands of Mr. Abbiss was keenly contested and eagerly watched by a very merry crowd. A Smelling Competition was a novelty introduced by Mrs. Davies and if not altogether easy diagnosing the contents of twelve bottles by the smell, it was certainly amusing watching others trying to do so.

Tea was a great feature of the afternoon and the rush was so great to the lawn under the large and stately cedar tree where tea was served that this department was taxed to the very utmost of its powers and even beyond it for a little while.

At 2.30, a large company gathered at the head of the Lime Avenue under which the stalls were placed and the Vicar with a few words of explanation as to the Bazaar and a few historical facts as to the old Belfry Tower, which looked down upon them introduced Emily Lady Ampthill, who had very kindly consented to come and open the Bazaar. With a chatty little history of Bells in general and the part they had played in the life of Merry England and with cheery good wishes for the success of the Restoration of Flitwick Bells she declared the Bazaar open.

That the day was not only fine, but just during those hours when most needed was bright with sunshine was another element that made for success. As said at the first we look back upon it all with hearts full of gratitude and thanks to all far and near and they were not a few who worked and helped so nobly and so well and especially the great Ruler and Disposer of all things that the one fine sunny day of the week should be the day of our Bazaar.

Parish Magazine 1909

The Manor, Flitwick.

September

"Season of mists and mellow fruitfulness,
Close bosom-friend of the maturing sun;
Conspiring with him how to load and bless
With fruit the vines that round the thatch-eves run;
To bend with apples the moss'd cottage trees,
And fill all fruit with ripeness to the core;
To swell the gourd, and plump the hazel shells
With a sweet kernel; to set budding more,
And still more, later flowers for the bees,
Until they think warm days will never cease,
For Summer has o'er brimm'd their clammy cells."

John Keats

September

1 _____

2 _____

3 _____

4 _____

5 _____

*"In September after burning stubble
Ponds and streams begin to bubble."*

Flower Show Sports

The Greased Pig (given by Messrs. Keelvil and Weston, of Smithfield Market) which was to become the property of the lady who succeeded in catching it, caused a great deal of fun.

When released, the pig naturally took to the open country, and was followed as closely as the running powers of the competitors would permit. Everyone present pushed on as hard as possible, over hill and dale, to be in at the death, or I should say, at the catch if possible. At first piggie got quite surrounded, owing to the manoeuvres of its would be owners, but it easily again and again slipped through their fingers. At last it got right away from its pursuers with the exception of Mrs. G. Brinkler and Mrs. F. Vincent, who gained on it rapidly, and as it was ascending a bank threw themselves bodily upon it and entangled it in their dresses and then drew it forth in triumph. Thus with piggie in their arms loudly squeeking its disapproval and struggling violently, now became their joint property, they returned and made their way with their pig in their arms through the crowd, amidst great cheering and laughter.

Parish Magazine 1902

"This little pig went to market;
This little pig stayed at home;
This little pig had roast beef;
And this little pig had none;
And this little pig cried,
"Wee, wee, wee!"
All the way home."

6

7

8

9

10

September

11

12

13

14

15

Illness

The Schools were re-opened on Monday, but the attendance was far from satisfactory, in consequence of illness, and the counter-attraction of Greenfield "statty." The attendance on Tuesday was much better.

There are many cases of serious illness reported in this village during the last few days. No doubt the many bad smells that the passer-by cannot be oblivious to are a fruitful cause of much of it, one smell especially which is a great nuisance being noticed near the Midland station. If Flitwick is to become the health resort contemplated and spoken of sometime since, surely these things must be attended to by the authorities, and the Medical Officer's and Nuisance Inspector's attention should be immediately drawn to them. During the last fortnight numerous complaints have been heard with regard to these smells.
Bedfordshire Times 1899

Smelly Business

For several years the matter of the traffic in London manure into Flitwick Station has caused discussions in the place, raised chiefly by residents by whom the smell arising from the discharge and cartage of the manure is considered a nuisance. In years gone by, we understand, no such care was exercised in the selection, loading and packing of the manure as is done at present, under the eyes of an inspector, and that now there is no danger of infection. An objectionable smell is however created, which is especially resented by some of the inhabitants near the station.
Bedfordshire Times 1902

"Sneeze on a Monday, sneeze for danger;
Sneeze on a Tuesday, kiss a stranger;
Sneeze on a Wednesday, get a letter;
Sneeze on a Thursday, something better;
Sneeze on a Friday, sneeze for sorrow;
Sneeze on a Saturday, see your sweetheart to-morrow."

16

17

18

19

20

September

21 *St Matthew*

22

23

24

25

"Harvest! harvest hum! harvest home!
We've ploughed, we've sown,
We've reaped, we've mown.
Harvest home! harvest home!"

FLITWICK CHURCH

Harvest Thanksgiving Sunday

On Sunday September 16th, we held our special services of Thanksgiving for the ingathered Harvest and for all the temporal gifts and mercies with which God has blessed us.

The day was a very happy one to us and we trust that those who crowded our Church, filling the sixty extra chairs placed in the aisles and any available corner, also filled our Church with an aroma of real thankfulness which would ascend on High and be well pleasing to the great Giver of all good gifts.

The Decorations were very pretty representing the fruits of Harvest from every point of view and our best thanks are due to Miss Brooks and her band of workers who undertook them and also to those who so willingly offered for this purpose the best and fairest of their store.

In such a case it is not so much the gift but the nature of the gift and the way it is given. The love and self-denial may shine forth in the humble blackberry, the picking of which has cost time and pricks, as brightly as in the most luscious grape or peach.

On the following Monday the fruit and vegetables were sent to cheer the hearts of the inmates of Ampthill Workhouse who just now almost entirely consist of the old and feeble.

Parish Magazine 1900

"September blow soft
Till the fruits are in the loft."

26

27

28

St Michael 29

30

Mr. John Abbott.

A brief review of the life of Mr. John Abbott will not be out of place here now that he is retiring, after nearly 40 years of active service in our midst, as the head master of the Flitwick Schools. On the day he first opened school in the one room, for there was no Infants Department then, and that one room even considerably smaller than at the present, there were only 36 children and a staff composed of one pupil teacher. Since that September morning in 1872 when Mr. Abbott took charge of the 36 children there have passed through his hands no less than 1286 little ones. What has become of them all! In 1871 Mr. Abbott was married, so practically his years at Flitwick coincide with the years of his married life. Here his family were born, here they have grown up and from the rose and ivy covered little house of the school have they gone forth into the world and carved out their respective lives, and that too with considerable credit and success. And now the time has come to lay aside the duties, responsibilities and we may well add the worries to which he was called in 1872.

Parish Magazine 1911

Frederick Bell Lipscomb

The Rev. Frederick Bell Lipscomb, M.A., who fell asleep in Christ on Wednesday, Sept. 27th, aged forty-six, was a man whom to know was to love, respect, and admire. In 1894 he was presented by Major Brooks to Flitwick, when he brought his ripe experience to bear in all the various organisations of a country parish. The services were marked by a depth of devotion and reverence which must appeal to all. He was always anxious to support any work for his people's good, and to be considered indeed their servant for Christ's sake. His death was one of those sudden calls to the better life which so frequently summon God's workers to the paradise of His love. He was returning on his bicycle from a visit in connection with S.P.G., when a young horse, getting loose, ran out of its stall into the road, and knocked him to the ground. Though he lingered for nearly two days he never regained consciousness, and death was, we are assured, painless.

  At an early hour on Saturday last his body was borne from the vicarage to the village church where there was a special Eucharist at 8.30. The coffin was covered with choice flowers, tokens of love. At one o'clock the funeral service began, which was largely attended, both by his own people, and friends from far and near. Almost all the clergy of the deanery were present. The village choir sang with simple beauty some of his favoured hymns, and in the peaceful churchyard, close to the chancel, the form of one "whom we have loved yet lost awhile" was left sleeping "till the day dawn." May he rest in peace.

Parish Magazine 1899

October

"The curfew tolls the knell of parting day,
The lowing herd wind slowly o'er the lea,
The ploughman homeward plods his weary way,
And leaves the world to darkness and to me.

Now fades the glimmering landscape on the sight,
And all the air a solemn stillness holds,
Save where the beetle wheels his droning flight,
And drowsy tinklings lull the distant folds;

Save that from yonder ivy-mantled tower
The moping owl does to the moon complain
Of such as, wandering near her secret bower,
Molest her ancient solitary reign."

Thomas Gray

October

1

2

3

4

5

*"Rain from the East,
Will last three days at least."*

EAST END, FLITWICK.

The Coal Club

The Coal Club numbers 30 members who have been paying in regularly since Oct. 1st of last year. The tickets for this year's coal were given out on Sept. 17th. Mr. Brown, of East End, will this year supply us, and the order has been given for the best coal; this together with the unusually high price, will mean that the members will not be able to have so much coal as usually.

The advantage of membership is briefly this: (1) They pay in little sums and don't feel it so much. It thus encourages economy. (2) They get the best coal at much cheaper rate than if they bought it themselves. This year there will be a saving of 2d or 3d per cent. (3) They get a Bonus added to their payments.

Any fresh members will be welcome to join with us on the first Monday in Oct. for another year.

Parish Magazine 1900

"By the 1st of March the crows begin to search
By the 1st of April they are sitting still
By the 1st of May they are flown away
Creeping greedy back again
With October wind and rain."

_____ 6

_____ 7

_____ 8

_____ 9

_____ 10

October

11 _____

12 _____

13 _____

14 _____

15 _____

*"Fresh October brings the pheasant,
Then to gather nuts is pleasant."*

Football Club

During the last few years several Football Clubs have been started but their lives have been short, and their usefulness of little worth. Last autumn another club was launched and a speedy break up was naturally predicted for it. But the prophets of evil were false for once. It has lived a whole season, played a number of matches, kept well together, enjoyed itself, and given pleasure to others, and has a balance in hand, in fact it has been a success. Though a child in years it is a healthy and growing one. We believe at last we have a Club that has come to stay and going to flourish. The following facts are of interest. Captain, Mr J. Dillingham, Secretary and Treasurer, Mr S. Short, Committee; Messrs. R. Dillingham, W. Carr, Knibbs and W. Odell.

The match record for a new club, with the considerable difficulty many of the best players have in getting off to play, is not bad. Won 3, Drawn 3, lost 8. Many Clubs played were very formidable opponents.

Finance.- Donations £2 8s 9d. Members Subscriptions, £3 1s 0d. Expenses £5 8s 10½d Balance in hand, 10½d.

Parish Magazine 1904

*"In October dung your field,
And your land its wealth shall yield."*

_____ 16

_____ 17

_____ *St Luke* 18

_____ 19

_____ 20

October

21

22

23

24

25

*"If the oak wears its leaves in October,
There will be a hard winter."*

Football

One of the most important fixtures of the season was played on Saturday on the Recreation Ground, when Maulden, who are old rivals, were the visitors. The home team were not well represented, although good substitutes were found on the field, whilst Maulden also were not at full strength. Flitwick won the toss and claimed the advantage of the sun and wind, and so much did they make of this that during the first half the ball was over the halfway line only thrice, whilst they forced no less than ten corners. But they failed to pierce the stubborn defence, and their shooting lacked judgment, with the result that they could not register a single point. Stapleton was exceedingly useful with his runs, but had his match in Phillips, who prevented him from carrying out his designs. After the interval the homesters again attacked, but were gradually forced to midfield. Here Kirby was noticeable for his dashes down the Maulden wing, from one of which the only goal of the match was scored. He sent in a shot which the custodian saved by fisting out, but Taylor being well up sent the ball back into the net.

Ampthill & District News 1900

*"A good October and a good blast
To blow the hog, acorn and mast."*

26

27

28

29

30

Hallow e'en 31

The Recreation Ground

As another landmark has now been reached in the life of our Recreation Ground, it may not be out of place to briefly review its history. The Village Cricket Club used to play in the field known as The Stockings, the plain English form of the old name "La Stockingge" by which it is alluded to in a document as far back as 1269. But this being none too convenient a general wish for a better ground was voiced by Mr. W. Baker, the Captain of the Club, and others. Major Brooks cordially fell in with the idea and offered the three acres which form our present ground, on Jan 5th 1889.

The preparation of the field was at once set in hand. It was divided off by a fence and a gate was placed in the corner leading to the road. Meeting after meeting was held, and a most elaborate code of Bye-laws was framed and set up. Every emergency seemed duly provided for. I quote a few by way of example:- "No person shall wilfully or carelessly throw or discharge in or into the ground any stone or other missile." "No person shall bring, or cause to be brought, any dog into the ground unless such dog shall be, and continue to be, under proper control." "No person shall in any part of the ground beat, shake, sweep, brush, or cleanse, any carpet, mat or any other fabric." "No person shall deliver any address in any part of the ground."

July 15th of the same year was a great and gay red-letter day, when the ground was opened by Lord Charles Russell, who made an excellent speech on "Progress" which was afterwards printed. To cricketers he gave this advice: "Play with a straight bat, never take your eyes off the ball and keep the right foot firm."

In succeeding years various efforts were tried to continue it as a success, but, as in many similar ventures, interest at last began to flag, the yearly income grew less and less, and the continual damage to fixtures, hedges, etc., kept the bills high, while subscriptions dropped off. If only that bye-law "No person shall enter or leave the ground except through the gates" had been kept the Committee would probably not have felt bound to give up the ground. On September 29th, 1912, it passed out of their hands, and the Parish Council, under slightly fresh conditions, have taken it over. We wish it still a career of usefulness and prosperity in the fullest meaning of its name "The Village Recreation Ground."

Parish Magazine 1912

Therefore each Flitwick girl and boy
Deserves congratulation,
For they will very soon enjoy
A ground for recreation.

CHURCH END, FLITWICK, (from the Hill.) We are staying 10 min walk from here.

November

"If I should die, think only this of me:
That there's some corner of a foreign field
That is forever England. There shall be
In that rich earth a richer dust concealed;
A dust whom England bore, shaped, made aware,
Gave, once, her flowers to love, her ways to roam,
A body of England's, breathing English air,
Washed by the rivers, blest by suns of home.

And think, this heart, all evil shed away,
A pulse in the eternal mind, no less
Gives somewhere back the thoughts by England given;
Her sights and sounds; dreams happy as her day;
And laughter, learnt of friends; and gentleness,
In hearts at peace, under an English heaven."

Rupert Brooke

November

1 *All Saints*

2 *All Souls*

3

4

5 *Guy Fawkes*

*"Remember, remember the fifth of November,
Gunpowder, treason, and plot."*

Windmill

The old windmill that for 60 years has been such a landmark at Denel End, and given the name to Windmill Road, was burnt to the ground in the small hours of the morning of November 10th. Most of the adjoining sheds near shared its fate. Unfortunately a horse, in spite of gallant attempts at rescue, was also burnt to death. The fire burnt so fiercely and rapidly that in spite of willing help there was scarcely time or chance to do anything. A sow and 8 pigs were luckily saved from a terrible death. The Ampthill Fire Brigade could only save the fire from spreading to the houses near. The origin of the fire is unknown.

Parish Magazine 1903

"No warmth, no cheerfulness, no healthful ease,
No comfortable feel in any member –
No shade, no shine, no butterflies, no bees,
No fruits, no flowers, no leaves, no birds, -
November!"

Thomas Hood

_____ 6

_____ 7

_____ 8

_____ 9

_____ 10

November

11

12

13

14

15

*"November's sky is chill and drear,
November's leaf is red and sear."*

The War

A great tempest of war is raging over the whole of Europe. England in honour bound and for her own safety has had to take her part in it. Terrible beyond expression, even beyond thought, we as a nation did all we could to avoid it. Now we must lay it in prayer before the God of Battles, and each must do his best in bearing burdens which fall and will fall so heavily and bitterly on many shoulders, it may be on our own. Our hearts are full of it as well as our papers. May the dark cloud that makes us realize things as never before speak in solemn voice to each one of us. May the fiery furnace open our eyes to our sins, to our need of a great conversion, and of a Saviour, and the pardon, comfort and help He only can give.

Parish Magazine 1914

*"They shall grow not old, as we that are left grow old.
Age shall not weary them, nor the years condemn.
At the going down of the sun and in the morning
We will remember them."*

_____ 16

_____ 17

_____ 18

_____ 19

_____ 20

November

21

22

23

24

25

*"Ice in November to bear a duck,
The rest of winter'll be slush and muck."*

The Volunteer Movement

The youths of Flitwick were given a splendid opportunity on Friday evening to show their patriotism by coming to the country's help at the present crisis, when a meeting was held in the Schoolroom for the purpose of raising a section of volunteers in the parish in connexion with the Ampthill Company – Major Brooks was in the chair, and was supported by Captain du Santoy, the officer commanding the Ampthill detachment. The meeting was of a free and easy description, and while the dangers of the empire and the need for its further defence were being fully considered the fragrant weed was placidly puffed by the numerous representatives of Flitwick's young blood, who had turned out at the call of duty, whilst convivial songs lent additional pleasure to the occasion.

    The Chairman led off, and spoke of the duties of every British subject at the present moment, and he hoped there would be a good number of Flitwick young men who would respond to the call for recruits for the volunteer movement. During his speech he referred to his military experiences, especially in the Indian Mutiny, which he said was the most enjoyable and exciting period of his whole life. Those present were then invited to give in their names, when eight were definitely promised and some others went home to "ask their Mammies."

Ampthill & District News 1900

"St Andrew the King
Three weeks and three days before Christmas comes in."

26

27

28

29

St Andrew 30

Flitwick Chalybeate Company

Two or three miles south of Ampthill, and surrounded by the parishes of Steppingley, Westoning, Tingrith, Eversholt, Flitton and Maulden lies the parish of Flitwick, occupying on the north a stretch of hilly Lower Greensand and on the south a long – once boggy – moor that reaches from Westoning to Flitton. The higher part of the parish consists largely of superficial strata of gravel, and of sands. The latter, some of which are perfectly white, and others of various shades of yellow, form the material of an important trade, the Flitwick sands finding ready sale for many purposes. The moor or bog was formerly dug for turf; but having been drained, most of it is now under plough or spade culture or laid down to pasture. To botanists Flitwick moor is interesting as being still the home of several rare plants which modern agriculture has in most places "cultivated out of existence." It is to be hoped that the enclosure of a large slice of the boggy part of the moor, in connexion with the Flitwick Chalybeate Springs will have the result of saving these rare plants from extermination in the locality.

The chalybeate character of the springs in question was discovered by the late Mr. Stevens, who for many years devoted himself to the development of the trade of this medicinal water. After the death of Mr. Stevens that land and proprietary rights were bought by a London firm of aerated water manufacturers who now trading under the name of Flitwick Chalybeate Company, place the water on the market for medicinal use. This water which flows from the iron-impregnated peat of the bog differs from other chalybeates in not readily depositing its iron as a precipitate, in the presence of a vegetable acid and other peat products, and in possessing a decidedly agreeable flavour. The area connected with the springs maintains much of its wild condition and is largely covered with self sown silver birches and rough herbage; but the springs themselves are now enclosed within high fences, in connexion with large iron buildings for the storing and preparation of the water, and are not open to public inspection.

Bedfordshire Times & Independent 1901

December

"In the bleak mid-winter
Frosty wind made moan,
Earth stood hard as iron,
Water like a stone;
Snow had fallen, snow on snow,
Snow on snow,
In the bleak mid-winter
Long ago."

Christina Rossetti

December

1

2

3

4

5

*"Cold December hath come in,
Poor people's backs are clothed thin,
The trees are bare, the birds are mute,
A pot of toast would very well suit."*

School Board

The last meeting of the old Board took place on Dec. 9th. Only two were present, Major Brooks and Mr. Cook. Strangely enough these are the only two members who have served continually ever since the formation of a Board in 1872 and have shared between them from that date the office of Chairman of which time Major Brooks held office for 28 years.

Of the ten Boards, each of three years office, there has only been one contested election. Mr. Abbott is the only teacher who was present at both the birth and death of the Flitwick Board. On the day of the first Board Meeting there were 36 children at School, on the day of the last there were 200.

Parish Magazine 1904

Postman

Mr. John Dalley was presented with a purse of gold on December 3rd, on his retirement, by the parishes of Flitwick and Steppingley, where for 33 years he has been postman. On a rough calculation he has done on his round some two hundred thousand miles. During this time he has won and deserved the confidence and respect of all. When he first started and for some years he could hold all his letters in one hand but it is very different now.

Parish Magazine 1910

"Deck the halls with boughs of holly,
'Tis the season to be jolly."

St Nicholas 6

7

8

9

10

December

11 _____

12 _____

13 _____

14 _____

15 _____

"Christmas is coming, the geese are getting fat,
Please put a penny in the old man's hat.
If you haven't got a penny, a ha'penny will do,
If you haven't got a ha'penny, God bless you!"

St. Thomas' Day

Not only is December 21st St Thomas Day and the shortest day, but it is the day on which Major Brooks very kindly distributes a hundred shillings to a hundred of the deserving poor. Ever since 1863 have they trooped up to the Manor and received at his hands the same sum. Even this date did not mark the beginning of what is now regarded as quite one of our parochial events. How many are there who can remember going up to the Manor on St. Thomas' Day, 1818 and receiving their gift from T.J. Brooks Esq., the Major's father?

    We wish to give a hearty "thank you" to the Squire for his kindness, and that it has been so long continued should make it all the heartier.

Parish Magazine 1900

*"St Thomas grey, St Thomas grey,
The longest night and the shortest day."*

_____ 16

_____ 17

_____ 18

_____ 19

_____ 20

December

21 *St Thomas*

22

23

24

25 *Christmas Day*

> *"Good tidings we bring,*
> *To you and your kin,*
> *We wish you a merry Christmas*
> *And a happy new year."*

Sunday School Treat

The Sunday School treat organized by Mr. Abbott on December 28th was a great success. First came the tea, then after a song or two by the children and various games. All this came as a prelude to the Christmas Tree which bore fruit of every variety and sufficient quantity for every child to have a share, and for those who had been most regular and well behaved to have a double portion. The tea was provided from half the proceeds of a concert arranged by the joint efforts of Mr. Stannard and Mr. Hawtin, and from a gift from Mrs. E. Abbiss, the result of a "Social" held early in the year. The fruit of the Christmas Tree was kindly and generously given by a number of friends. The arrival of Father Christmas in the well disguised person of Mr. A. Ayling was greeted with loud cheering and caused a great deal of merriment, and many a one carried away some of the "Snow" from his flowing garments as a memento of the occasion. Hearty thanks and lusty cheers were given for Mr Abbott and all the kind friends, Teachers and Helpers, also for the Vicar and Father Christmas.

Parish Magazine 1907

> "If on New Year's eve the wind blows south
> It betokeneth warmth and growth;
> If west, much milk and fish in the sea,
> If north, cold and storms there will be;
> If west, the trees will bear much fruit,
> If north-east, then flee it, man and beast."

St Stephen **26**

27

Holy Innocents Day **28**

29

30

31

The Girls' Friendly Society

At the annual gathering the Fairy Play, "The Sleeping Beauty" was the chief feature. The performers were almost all chosen from the G.F.S. candidates and the greatest credit is due to Miss Burridge, who had taken such infinite pains in training the little ones and dressing them which in itself was no small task. Miss Van Toll presided at the piano.

The parts were as follows - Sleeping Beauty, A. Fowler, The Prince, E.Deacon, The Queen, R.Vincent, The King, M. Denton, The Nurse, A. Harriss, Fairies, J. Edgecombe, R. Chapman, M. and F. Kenealy, M. and L. Jellis, E. Hannuell, E. Webb, R.Virgin. It was a pleasant sight to see the joy of the little ones and their singing and dancing was remarkably good. It was received with well deserved applause. Songs were given afterwards by Miss Brooks and the Misses Spencer who also gave a most amusing dialogue "The Jumble Sale." Miss Brooks kindly invited all to tea.

Parish Magazine 1904

A thing of beauty is a joy for ever:
Its loveliness increases; it will never
Pass into nothingness; but it will keep
A bower quiet for us, and a sleep
Full of sweet dreams, and health, and quiet breathing.

John Keats

Notes

January

Front	Postcard from the Blake & Edgar "Picturesque Bedfordshire" series, featuring; Church Road, Church Hill, St Peter and St Paul Parish Church, High Street and Flitwick Railway Station.
1-10	Postcard featuring; Flitwick Railway Station, the school, Flitwick Manor gardens, Flitwick Manor and St Peter and St Paul Parish Church.
11-20	Postcard of the village school at Church End.
21-31	Postcard of St Peter and St Paul Parish Church.

February

Front	Postcard from the Blake & Edgar "Picturesque Bedfordshire" series of Flitwick Church.
1-10	Postcard from the Valentine's Series featuring cartoon by Louis Wain.
11-20	Postcard of the village school, the village blacksmith occupied the building on the right.
21-29	Postcard of the Manor Grounds owned by the Brooks family until 1934. In the foreground is the lake used by the villagers for skating.

March

Front	Postcard from the Blake & Edgar "Picturesque Bedfordshire" series of The Mill, Flitwick, owned by the Goodman family for over three centuries.
1-10	Photograph of the Cookery Class at Greenfield School in the next village along the road from Flitwick Mill.
11-20	Photograph of Kate (Pedder) Virgin, on right of picture, in service at a residence in Chapel Road.
21-31	Family photograph of Kate Virgin with children Violet and James.

April

Front	Painting "The Vale Farm, Flitwick, Beds." by Henry John Sylvester Stannard.
1-10	Postcard of St. Andrew's church, built in 1903 to serve the expanding community at Denel End.
11-20	Postcard of Flitwick Wesleyan church, built at Denel End in 1873.
21-30	Postcard of "Ampthill Road" but actually showing the shops in the High Street at Denel End. The Wheatsheaf public house is on the right of the picture.

May

Front	Rush & Warwick postcard of High Street, Flitwick.
1-10	Postcard featuring a painting by H. Stannard.
11-20	Postcard of The Avenue with the Post office at the centre.
21-31	Photograph of Flitwick cricket team of 1921 taken on the Recreation ground, the houses in the background are in Station Square.

June

Front	Postcard from the Blake & Edgar "Picturesque Bedfordshire" series of The Vicarage, Flitwick residence of the Revd. and Mrs Petley from 1900 to 1927.
1-10	Postcard of Flitwick Station looking north towards Bedford. The goods yard to the left unusual in that it was situated on the west side rather than the east of the Midland railway line.
11-20	Postcard of Church End.
21-30	Postcard of Flitwick Station

July

Front	Postcard from the Blake & Edgar "Picturesque Bedfordshire" series of Flitwick Station opened in 1870, two years after the opening of the line from Bedford to London.
1-10	Photograph of the gardens of Flitwick Manor.
11-20	Postcard of The Old Lodge, Flitwick Manor at the end of Church Hill. A second lodge was situated on the Westoning road.
21-31	Photograph of children outside the parish church lychgate.

August

Front	Postcard from the Blake & Edgar "Picturesque Bedfordshire" series "A bit of old Flitwick" showing the cottages in Church Road at the bottom of Church Hill.
1-10	Postcard entitled "The Race" dated 1904.
11-20	A class photograph of Flitwick School in 1915. Headmaster Thomas Strickland is seen standing on the right.
21-31	Photograph of the cottages in Church Road that were destroyed by fire in the 1930's.

September

Front	Postcard of The Manor, Flitwick.
1-10	Early postcard posted in Leipzig in 1901.
11-20	Photograph of haymaking at Folly Farm on the edge of Flitwick Moor. The owner Mr King Stephens is standing at the centre of the picture. It was he who discovered and exploited the healing qualities of "Flitwick Water"
21-30	Postcard showing the interior of Flitwick Church at the turn of the century.

October

Front	Postcard from the Blake & Edgar "Picturesque Bedfordshire" series of Church Hill, Flitwick.
1-10	Postcard of East End, Flitwick showing cottages in Station Road and the White Horse public house. Maulden Road is in the distance.
11-20	Photograph of Flitwick Football Club, season 1919-1920.
21-31	Photograph of village coach party outside the Blackbirds Inn about to leave for the races. Thomas Virgin is 6th from the right.

November

Front	Postcard from the Blake & Edgar "Picturesque Bedfordshire" series of Church End Flitwick, from the Hill. This was the view from what is today Vicarage Hill. The village school is directly behind the tree.
1-10	Photograph of the windmill in Denel End on the site of Common Farm formerly in Windmill Road.
11-20	Postcard of the War Memorial bearing the names of 29 men of Flitwick killed in action during World War One.
21-30	Photograph of the Revd. J. L. Ward Petley at the dedication service of the War Memorial in 1922.

December

Front	Painting of Church End by W. Dillamore dated 1923.
1-10	Postcard of the Manor House Flitwick with the village postman in the foreground.
11-20	Photograph of Thomas (Paraffin Tom) Virgin alongside his horse and cart used for delivering paraffin and other house wares to local inhabitants.
21-31	Christmas greetings card from the collection of Kate Virgin 1906.
Back	Postcard featuring Ampthill Road, Church Hill, Running Waters, the mill and church.

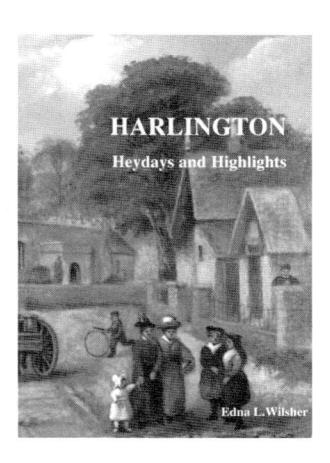

HARLINGTON
HEYDAYS AND HIGHLIGHTS
Edna L. Wilsher

A journey on a golden September afternoon in 1996 from her home in Silsoe to Harlington, Bedfordshire, the village of her birth, awakened the author's memories to past events in her life. Harlington's connections with the evangelist, John Bunyan are featured, linking with her own early childhood when she attended the village school by the church.

The quiet little village came alive with the arrival of evacuees from London at the beginning of the war, thereafter never to be the same again. Her own journalistic career at Home Counties Newspapers was put on hold when she was called into the Auxiliary Territorial Service, stationed in London with V1 and V2 bombs falling all around, and nostalgic thoughts of Harlington crossed her mind, although it, too, had its own wartime traumas.

Historical pageantry came with the opening of the new village hall, returning again for its fiftieth anniversary celebrations. The millennium is also highlighted.

After marriage, the author became a freelance writer for national magazines. Her inspiration for this story was drawn from a very special award-winning painting, featured on the cover of this book.

A Book Castle Publication

GLEANINGS REVISITED
Nostalgic Thoughts of a Bedfordshire Farmer's Boy
E.W.O'Dell

The original small town of Barton has gradually spread and grown over the years. Very few of the current residents can still recall the way of life there in days gone by. However, here one of the few collected his thoughts and embellished them with his own sketches, plus early photographs. These are not always idyllic memories, but they are real, they are lively and they give an insight into rural Bedfordshire as many once experienced it – at work, rest and play.

A Book Castle Publication

THREADS OF TIME
Shela Porter

A pale-faced city child is evacuated from London during the Zeppelin raids of 1917. In Hitchin she takes a dressmaking apprenticeship and opens her own workshop with customers including the local gentry and the young Flora Robson.

Moving to Bedford on her marriage, her sewing skills help her rapidly growing family to survive the Depression; working long hours during the exigencies of war-time Britain, it is her re-designed battle-jacket that Glenn Miller is wearing when he disappears over the Channel in 1944, and entertainers Bing Crosby and Bob Hope leave comics and candy for her 'cute kids'. For five years after the war the family run a small café in the town but sewing then sees her through again as the business is sold, she is widowed with a nine-year-old son to raise, all her children gradually leave and she moves away to be wardrobe mistress to a big operatic society in High Wycombe. Finally she settles in a small cottage opposite the great airship sheds at Cardington from where she once watched the ill-fated R101 take off on its last journey in 1930.

A mirror of her times, this gripping biography tells the story of a remarkable lady, a talented dressmaker, mostly in Hitchin and Bedford - played out against the unfolding drama of the entire twentieth century.

A Book Castle Publication

BEDFORDSHIRE'S YESTERYEARS VOL 2
The Rural Scene
Brenda Fraser-Newstead

Social history comes to life, first-hand and vivid, when seen through the eyes of those who experienced and shaped it.

To bring us a taste of the early twentieth century, the author has collated the recollections of a wide variety of our longest-surviving local residents.

The 'Bedfordshire's Yesteryears' series contains many privileged glimpses of a way of life that has changed radically. Here is the generation of two World Wars; here are the witnesses to countless technological and sociological transformations.

This volume concentrates on country and farm life- from humble cottage to big house. Here is the village in all its interlinking relationships and facets – the farm with its unique demands and customs – all enlivened by special rural pleasures and celebrations.

A Book Castle Publication

JOHN BUNYAN
His Life and Times
Vivienne Evans

Born to a humble family in the parish of Elstow near Bedford, John Bunyan (1628-1688) became one of the world's most widely read Christian writers – The Pilgrim's Progress eventually being translated into over two hundred languages.

This lively book traces the events of his life with its spiritual turmoil and long imprisonment, as well as discussing many of his writings. Clearly seeing Bunyan as a product of his time and place, it also explains the intriguing social, political and religious background of the turbulent seventeenth century.

A Book Castle Publication

LOCAL WALKS NORTH AND MID-BEDFORDSHIRE
Vaughan Basham

A comprehensive book of circular walks in this lovely rural area - a companion to the same author's collection of walks in South Bedfordshire and the North Chilterns.

Walking in the countryside is always enjoyable, but, with this book as his companion, the rambler will also be led to many interesting discoveries. An appropriate theme has been selected for every walk, and a stimulating introductory article sets the scene.

Full practical route information and comments are also provided, plus specially drawn maps.

An appendix of further walking areas includes the author's suggestions for two new long-distance circular walks.

The author, Vaughan Basham, has lived in and explored the area all his life. His keen interest in social history has led to a continuing involvement in heritage affairs, conservation projects, local organisations and charities. Scouting and the Outward Bound schools were influential in his love of the countryside and, together with his wife Una, he has always been an enthusiastic rambler.

A Book Castle Publication